MIDNIGHT BESTIARIES

Andre Bagoo is a poet, writer, essayist, and visual artist. He lives in Trinidad with his dog, Chaplin.

Also by Andre Bagoo

POETRY

Narcissus	(Broken Sleep Books, 2022)
Writing through Siddhartha	(Broken Sleep Books, 2021)
The City of Dreadful Night	(Hesterglock, 2018)
Pitch Lake	(Peepal Tree, 2017)
BURN	(Shearsman, 2015)
Trick Vessels	(Shearsman, 2012)

PROSE

The Dreaming	(Peepal Tree, 2022)
The Undiscovered Country	(Peepal Tree, 2020)

Midnight Bestiaries

Andre Bagoo

Broken Sleep Books

© 2024, Andre Bagoo. All rights reserved; no part of this book may be reproduced by any means without the publisher's permission.

ISBN: 978-1-916938-45-8

The author has asserted their right to be identified as the author of this Work in accordance with the Copyright, Designs and Patents Act 1988

Cover designed by Aaron Kent

Edited and Typeset by Aaron Kent

Broken Sleep Books Ltd
PO BOX 102
Llandysul
SA44 9BG

CONTENTS

IN WHICH WE ARE AFRAID

BESTIARY SET AT THE LIVE DRAWING SESSION	11
SEASON OF THE JAGUAR	12
BESTIARY IN WHICH I HAVE OFTEN BEEN WRONG	14
BESTIARY IN WHICH I UGLY CRY AT THE ZOOM READING	15
BESTIARY IN WHICH I AM STALKED BY A CAT	18
BESTIARY IN WHICH I HAVE NOTHING LEFT ANYMORE	20
BESTIARY SET ON BOXING DAY	23
BESTIARY IN WHICH I FIT INTO HIS ARMS PERFECTLY	25
SOMETIMES I LOOK AT MY EX-BOYFRIENDS' SOCIAL MEDIA PROFILES IN ORDER THAT I MAY LAUGH AT THEM	26
BESTIARY SET IN THE PORT OF SPAIN GENERAL HOSPITAL	27
DUNGENESS	29
PROSPECT COTTAGE, 2022	30
BESTIARY WITH SPY WHALE	32
THE JAGUAR	33
THE RIVER OF DOUBT	34
ON THE HATRED OF V.S. NAIPAUL	35

THE CREATURE IN THE FLOWERS

CHAPTER I	39
CHAPTER II	49
CHAPTER III	59
CHAPTER IV	65
CHAPTER V	73
CHAPTER VI	81

ACKNOWLEDGEMENTS	93

Tonight, which shall I be for you?
Otter, bear, wolf, or nasty pig? I am your dream of
beasthood. I am your snouted creature. I am your life

on all fours like the hunter turned by a vengeful god into a
stag with antlers yearning to the eucharist moon.

This world is not conclusion, my species stands beyond.

If I am dreamt, dream me thus: your acolyte, your emissary,
bearing your hot missives through snares of sharp stubble,

through the razor grass cut of insect lust. Dream my long
eyelashes – my last human touch – as I root and root
into buried need set free, at last, by the mask I wear,

by the spiked urgings of Carnival standards
that tear my past like the claws of a dog

whose neck is as soft as the skin of the man I love.

Eventually,
we dream the real.

In Which We Are Afraid

BESTIARY SET AT THE LIVE DRAWING SESSION

It falls from the sky, this innocence, this unfinished lifework I didn't know I needed in my life. It falls onto the table, falls into my sketchpad, sculpted torso dreaming of its own ekphrasis, a fragment completing itself: perfect shoulders, perfect legs, perfect trail of hair along a perfect chest that glows from within like a hurricane lamp and then, too, the addition of the placid penis, relishing its own flesh, cushioned sacs engorged with seeds of love. Is it love? Once, I played a lamb in a nativity play and the angel had a crown of gold straw. Now, what stands before me is a puma. Or at least that is what I see when I stare into his eyes and he stares back at me. He is not what I see but what I am. What I draw, I become. All his poses seem to say: Even when things don't work out, they work out but only as long as you don't give up, as long as you don't stop sketching me, just as the body must succumb to its own illusion, from moment to moment, the self imagining self, somehow residing between ears and behind eyes. I see in his face a lion but also, in the gentle cascade of his limbs, a gazelle. Then it falls from the ceiling, the zandolie – as small as a teardrop, and I take a piece of paper and scoop it up and carry it out the front door. Here, there is no angle from which you are not seen. You must not give up.

SEASON OF THE JAGUAR

In the year of the jaguar, in the month of the jaguar, in the week when residents of Palo Seco whispered about it, when a lady said forest rangers approached her warning it was on the prowl, when mothers were frightened for their children, when homeowners worried about their dogs in the yard, when the gas company at Orinoco Drive told residents it was pigging a pipeline (in this industry there are many types of pigs: utility pigs, mandrel pigs, solid cast pigs, foam pigs, spherical pigs, gel pigs, inspection pigs, speciality pigs), and the jaguar was not seen for two whole days, and residents said the dog Lucy had been bitten and no one saw and there was talk of a big cat at the bridge and no one saw and a boy was going to the shop and he saw a big black cat with white eyes and game wardens visited but left empty handed and yet somehow the idea of the notion of the possibility that the jaguar had been smuggled in from Venezuela took flight and an acting corporal and a police constable from the Santa Flora Police Station as well as three constables from the South West Division Task Force went searching. The beast left behind no paw prints, no photos, no videos only aura raga ajar jar jug rag jag. Yet a few days before, on May 31, police got a tip-off and went to a location miles away in northwest Trinidad, where they seized a jaguar cub and exotic birds from an abandoned campsite. The animals were believed to have been smuggled. The cub was handed over to the Emperor Valley Zoo. The Minister of Agriculture, Land and Fisheries visited the juvenile, and the Conservator of Forests visited the juvenile. A year before, no four years before, another jaguar had been surrendered to the zoo. Intelligence sources had said two jaguars had been smuggled in, but one died. Maybe it is this one that keeps roaming the country. There is a book, compiled by many hands, of lost beasts left to their fate in the Flood, beasts refused entry to the Ark by Noah when he set sail in the Great Flood. Many times has the book surfaced and been lost and surfaced and been lost and men have died searching for it, though by the year 1255 it was said to have disappeared forever. We have always been imaginary.

BESTIARY IN WHICH I HAVE OFTEN BEEN WRONG

A few weeks later, I dream the bird is not dead. I dream it is alive and lives in a mall downtown. I dream it has grown large, the size of a turkey really, and has a long beak, like a puppet in a Jim Henson show, and has no feathers, is buzzed, and speaks to say it is living in a bucket. The mall is half-empty, a nest that has long been abandoned, and there is a corridor that opens onto the pavement on Chacon Street, where everything is covered in grease, as though the whole street is a giant parking lot where the same car each day leaks oil. I dream that I wake up and the moon sits like a broken button against the pale blue fabric of the air. And Buster, yet again, thinks there is another animal in the yard, is convinced there is an animal in the yard. There is nothing in the yard. And yet he runs from one ghost to the next. I dream this and think, as I imagine it, how sad it is to believe in something, how sad it is to be wrong. Or is it that belief is more real than what is real, that Buster is right, and the bird is really there? When it comes to Buster, I have often been wrong. I have often reprimanded him for barking at nothing, only to find an iguana shading under the old rusty galvanise in the yard, its claws like a falcon's talons.

BESTIARY IN WHICH I UGLY CRY AT THE ZOOM READING

Maybe it's like the day I first met you, when a
fledgling fell out of its nest, and I didn't notice
until Buster found it, dogsniffed it, lolloped and
dawdled around it, and, with his forepaws, dabbed the
small thing as though testing some flame he had just
created. That day, I discovered three things: Buster's
desperate need for a playmate other than me; the
beauty and vulnerability of a fledgling that could never
really give Buster what he needed; and the nest that
had been built, clandestinely, behind the air
conditioning unit of the empty apartment next door, a
nest built by a pair of brown doves I never saw, who
had constructed their secret, stick by stick, leaf by
leaf, as though love itself was agglomeration. I held
Buster back so he wouldn't harm the little bird, that
looked like a cross between a wet moth and a tiny bat,
and then I quickly went inside to google what to do
when a bird falls out of a nest. The solution was not to
move it but to leave it: the parents would, most likely,
be nearby and they would need to know where it was.
I went back to the yard outside. One parent was in the
nest, guarding the other fledglings. The other was on
the wall at the far end of the yard, staring straight at
me. They had been staring all along. I left the bird
where it was and went back inside. And sure enough,
when I peeped out of the window a half hour later,
there was a bold parent, shielding its child with one of its

wings. (This act of shielding, I would later learn, is identical to the act of what birdwatchers call 'mantling', which is what a bird does to conceal dead prey.) I didn't know then that most birds that fall out of their nest will die not from exposure to the elements, not from predators, not for want of food, not from abandonment by parents, but from the simple fact of gravity, from the blunt impact of falling. And they die alone.

The next day when I go into the yard, the fledgling will be dead, will be shrunken into a mere twig, as though the soul (?) is a physical thing that must be accommodated by the body and, once removed, what is left is a crinkled moult. And I will think I should write a poem about this. But you will want to meet again, so I won't write. Yet, in the café as we chat, I will think about reading that much-discussed book *The Peregrine.* And I will remember the season I spent my days doing nothing but writing a poem called 'The Scarlet Ibis'. The poem went on for pages and pages and it was written in syllabic verse but sometimes it would slip, and I wondered if it was really a poem or a novel or a verse novel and what did such things mean? What did it all mean? The text imagined the flight of a lone bird over the Caroni Swamp, mangroves unfolding beneath like the undulating waves of the sea, over the vast green whale of the Northern Range, over the city of Port of Spain, over the ever-changing collage of roofs below. We change. Eventually, this bird ends up in the hospital and becomes me and isn't that what all birdwatchers wish to do, become one with their obsession? And even though I had spent so long on this abandoned poem, I realised that I never really knew this bird, never really knew *any* bird, if I can ever know one. And that very night, when I am alone after spending the rest of the day with you before your departure, I cry during the Zoom reading I attend when someone reads a poem about a sparrow and I think back to all the birds and you and me and how my life is now pierced by something and I can neither move forward nor backward even as I move forward and backward, even as I am in this country and your country, even as I am the case and am not the case, veering between a poem and a novel, a short story and an epic, writing myself and being written. And I cannot tell what chapters are to unfold yet for me, which is to say, perhaps, us, and I cannot see the past nor can I see the future. I cannot even see the present (what is time?) I cannot see you anymore than I can see me, who is not this I. And still, I see everything, like the eldritch colours that only the scarlet ibis can see, that the brown dove can see, the sparrow can see.

BESTIARY IN WHICH I AM STALKED BY A CAT

This is the second time an animal has appeared in the yard and then vanished without a trace. The first was three weeks ago. I was walking Buster in the yard. We stood together braced against the wind. I had this feeling as though someone was staring at me. I looked up and there it was, on the roof of the small apartment next door. Nobody lives in that apartment. None of my neighbours owns a cat. It sat on the roof like a sphinx. The sun set behind it. Its eyes were alchemised. Buster was barking at it. I had to quickly take him back inside. I didn't like the idea of Buster fighting with a cat. When I came back outside, I made sure I'd secured our door carefully (Buster had learned how to open doors). The cat was gone. But the feeling of being watched remained. Then, last night, Buster and I were sleeping peacefully in bed, his soft fur against my leg. It was near midnight. Buster lept like a charger, barking. It was a different kind of bark. Buster barks a lot and I have learned to identify which bark means what. This bark did not mean play with me or feed me or there is something annoying me or let me hump you or I don't like this person. This bark meant **I am afraid**. When I looked out the window, there was a cat on the neighbour's wall, staring straight in at us. I don't know if it was because I had been watching *The Haunting of Hill House* on Netflix, but I immediately felt my life was in imminent danger. Buster barked and barked and barked, each bark the echo of his self, but the cat did not budge. I thought about opening the window and throwing something at it. As though it had read my mind, the cat dug in its heels, peering deeper at us, its eyes lit by hate. I cannot say now if this was the same cat from three weeks prior. I cannot say for sure what it looked like, like if it had stripes. It seemed at one with the hostile wind. Buster never climbs up to the window, but he jumped up there faster than I could say no and barked even louder. I have never heard him bark as loud. After several minutes, the cat slowly tiptoed away on the wall. I went back to sleep, but Buster stayed at the base of the bed, looking out the window just in case. I woke up the next morning and decided I would kill the lover of the protagonist in my poem. And then I would bring him back to life as a cat. And he would haunt the hero. But the hero will never know and will write poems about the cat. When I quickly rushed to write all this down, two brown doves appeared outside my window, sitting on the same spot where the cat was. Several birds have died in my yard.

BESTIARY IN WHICH I HAVE NOTHING LEFT ANYMORE

It happened inside a single poem. We were Christmas
shopping and you saw a crocodile severed in

                two as though by a
magician. In those days, I was always looking for
bookends and this one was truly glorious, covered in
silver scales.
But it was hollow, despite the promise
of so much weight. Sometimes, that's what gets you,
not that something's not strong enough but that you
thought it would be and piled so many books unto it
only for it to all fall over like dominos.
I didn't want to write a Christmas poem because all my
Christmas poems are sad, but here I go again with
another one, another scene: this time we are stringing
lights on the Christmas tree and I realise you'll never
know who I am, really. Sometimes, that's what you get:
a string of lights that would be brilliant if all the bulbs
lit. But instead, half of them are sleeping and you have
to check hundreds, each its own snow globe, to figure
out where things have gone wrong. And sometimes you
never find the problem, and you must decide if you
should buy a new string or keep the old things, half lit
on the tree.

Now I wake from my second sleep,
and find the dead bat in the yard,
its skin the colour of a blackened mango

ripened too long, torn asunder by birds.
Some painter has circled it with blood,
A perimeter of aching that says:
Don't let them take my head,
and dance upon my grave.

When the day has been too long
and we roam the yard at night,
they fly past my head, a stream, a causeway,
roping together trees in yards like telephone lines.
Each grazes me, and for a moment I'm
back in the club, worried that I might be
touched by someone who knows
far more about me than I do;
worried that one day I might be free
of all of this

            failure, which is to say one day
I'll find the reason why I haven't given up.

There's a type of bird without feet, that never roosts
from the moment of its dropbirth until its
deathfall. All birds have feet and most have
four toes, three pointing forward and one back,
as though all directions are possible. But
let me, in this season, be a martlet
let me haunt temples
let me kiss heaven's masonry
let me bulb and become a nest myself
let bats envy my pendent bed, my procreant cradle

let me follow swifts
let me learn the delicacy of air
let me learn
let me forget

BESTIARY SET ON BOXING DAY

I never understood why we had turtles. Father made a special holding bay for them out of red clay bricks, half of which he filled with sand and gravel, the other half of which he turned into a small, shallow pond. In such confinement, the islands grew, each a mosaic of yellows and browns and blacks. Nothing was darker than their eyes. Part of the pen was covered with a metal grill so as to be shaded, the other half over the water was covered in chicken wire. Sometimes you'd see the turtles in the water, as if sunbathing. Other times they would mimic their pattern of nocturnal aggregation and clump together in the shade. Once, a white egg appeared, smooth as a Jordan almond. It never hatched. Mother would throw cabbage into the pen and sing the turtles songs. Father would top up the water in the pond. I never realised these turtles were us until it was too late. Each child in roles we never chose, life divided neatly into light and shadow; dry sand and water; fed and hungry – never free, yet, strangely, in this curtailment, masters of a world of our own. The day they told me the turtles had died I returned to my apartment. That was the third night the cat appeared on the wall. This time, when Buster barked, I looked out and could barely see it, to the extent that I questioned whether I saw it though he was adamant in his barking that it was there. I took out my phone and took a picture through the slender curtain. I put on my glasses. Thank you, good boy, I told Buster. He stopped barking. When I looked there was no cat. I must write my book, I thought. The next morning when I looked at the photo, it was a white image, like a blank page. In the mental disorder once called *folie à deux*, because you think someone else has seen something or because you yourself once saw something you can think you are seeing it too. Someone said an angry neighbour poisoned the turtles. We will never know for sure. I didn't think to ask what they did with the bodies.

BESTIARY IN WHICH I FIT INTO HIS ARMS PERFECTLY

Often, I think about a line from the play *A Streetcar Named Desire* in which Blanche says *Sometimes – there's God – so quickly!* and I think about how wrong Blanche was about her lovers. Water bridges all things, life and death; darkness and light. Maybe I fit into you the way water fills a tarn. That's a word in your name, tarn. Other words: sitar, satin, shirt. When I am with you the day feels like night, the night day. The afternoon feels more like the afternoon. I want to climb stairs with you. I want to walk through rain. I want to go to church and watch the saints in their robes. I want to dance in the club as bodies inch closer and closer. Another word in your name is tsar, but my favourite is *his*. I wake up on the first day of the new year and there's no light in the room and I nestle my head near your armpits. For the first time I think Blanche was not wrong. Because what is life if not a leap into the broken world? Buster crawls unto your side of the bed and curls up, the happiest of the mongrel race. I feel the slow movement of the mountains on the island, back to the Andes of South America, back to where they started. I hear a row of green parakeets outside the window, the parakeets that fly, each day, between two parks nearby. And I realise that from now on I'll never hide my dreams from you.

SOMETIMES I LOOK AT MY EX-BOYFRIENDS' SOCIAL MEDIA PROFILES IN ORDER THAT I MAY LAUGH AT THEM

I came late to the love of birds
There are scarlet ibises all over my friend's book
There are birds all over the hospital's wall
There are birds all over the birds
In the poem, the beast in the park is silent,
flowers are as fragile as roses in *The Innocents*
I've been recording thrushes again
You've written this before

BESTIARY SET IN THE PORT OF SPAIN GENERAL HOSPITAL

The end of the world will look like this

The building old as empire, yet the doctors so young

All I see: chipped ceilings, faded posters, the frailty of limbs

All I hear: squeaky doors, muffled announcements, the silence
    made by waiting

There is a real pigeon over   there

Nobody looks at it

Everyone looks like they've been sleeping in cars

A dog scratches in front the door saying ECHO

I wonder if life is a mystery you repeat

Like a barking dog flashing forth the

Flame of his very self (what does it mean to repeat?)

Or like the frequent movie scene with people huddling

After some disaster nobody saw coming

Yet everybody saw coming (heartbeats, repetition)

The light jumps up the wall like a cat

There's a whole family of kittens under this wing

They are tearing down the old wing

– that is, the wing older than this one –

To make way for something new (what does it mean to write?)

Some of these people will die and know it

Here, I was born

DUNGENESS

It is seaword. It is salt. It is thrashing of arms and legs in
dusk and low tide. It is the tern plunging into a wave to find
itself and yet not finding itself. It is the six "visual scores" of the
poet, the seven lighthouses, that must be retracted, revised, re-written,
like the shoals beneath history. There is a desert in
California where only marigolds grow. It is the idea of a desert,
for the Met Office now says that, too, is a fiction. It is the world
contracted thus: into an endless ocean of shingle, endlessly thrown up.
It is the world's smallest railway, that playfully calls to us as we sit
in The Pilot eating fish and chips. It is the pair of shells I take back
with me to London, to Walthamstow, where a split leaf marks the
entrance to the marshes, where cattle once grazed, where Althea
McNish is on display in the William Morris Gallery and I can
recognise the quality of the tropical light dappling every single
shrub and flower on her fabrics and I think of the way the smaller
shell fits into the bigger shell like a couple spooning and I wonder
if you will keep this memento. You had always wanted to visit Prospect
Cottage, you say, cupping the shell in your hand as though this
is where it was meant to be. It is the unruly sun, that fades the
writing on the cottage wall. It is the boiling water from the
nuclear plant, which, through subterranean currents, nourishes the
sea and brings the birds. It is the wave after each wave of realisation.
It is the thought. It is the hope: it is not too late. It is too late for us.

PROSPECT COTTAGE, 2022

a shelter
of the mind
against sky
against time
a cloister of
not-aloneness
that is
aloneness
blackness
becoming
not-blackness,
the half-dissolved
transparence
of wet dreams
in which arms
spread wide
like eaves opening
to let in gusts
that have come through sea
cold sea, low enigma
throwing up light
absorbed by tar
coating the cottage
that must open
a body being unlocked
a wanting to be inside
a wanting inside
to want is to be filled

and fringed with
lavender-cotton
evergreen
aromatic
against sky, button-like
flowerheads
saying
we have grown young
we have grown old
we are potpourri
we are reborn
of windows
of doors
and broken

    boats
anchoring
impermanence
little arks
galvanised chaos
in a watery
reduction of
the incondite world
the will to believe in
supernatural preludes
to floods

BESTIARY WITH SPY WHALE

I sprinkle salt along my windowsill to stop the slugs and yet still they cross the line, the way you can move from dream to waking life and still the dream can hold you, make you think you are married or the President or something else you will never be. The slimy em dashes become curled commas as I scoop them away and when later I read the article about the spy whale found off the coast of Sweden, I say to myself I must put that in the book I'm writing, along with the slugs. And when I stumble over Buster's toy serpent, which looks like it's fallen out of a game of snakes and ladders, I notice how it has the same ~ of the slugs and I say to myself I must put that in the book I'm writing. And when my sister calls, without warning, to say she's outside, I say to myself I must put that in the book I'm writing, too, though I no longer know why. There are some people who treat each day like a single life. There are writers who write just before bed. One definition for the novel is that it is set inside a dream. Each beluga whale has a spiracle, no fin, a head that is deformable. From space, the only animal visible is the whale. All white, I see it now, the one in my mind. In the article, someone speculates about why the whale is moving away from its natural environment, faster and faster. It could be hormones, he says. It could be loneliness. Maybe the dolphin no longer wants to be a dolphin, the way a dog does not wish to be a dog but rather something unnamed, unfound, something from the landscape's very beginning.

THE JAGUAR

In the photograph, the President kneels beside it. With one hand he holds a rifle. With the other he supports its head. It is not asleep. It is not dreaming. It is a sphinx in awkward repose, no longer poised, no longer painted on some child's nursery wall. This is savagery incarnate, under the guise of conservation. The underside of one paw exposed to the camera, eyes closed, yet teeth exposed, as though being made to smile at its own fate, to participate in this staging of masculinity, to take it and take it and take it and say Yes, Sir. Thank you, Sir. Thank you, Mr President. And all the while, rosettes bloom and multiply, each the smudge of a hawk roosting at the apex of the forest trees, each a bird in a row of birds on a power line in a polyglot city of no love, each an oil spill within the fabrications of industry, each a cell generating more cells, each a kernel of generations who have fallen prey and will yet fall prey to this man, who once boasted of going on a safari and killing nine lions, eight elephants, seven giraffes, three pythons, two ibises and a crocodile. It made our veins thrill, he wrote, this colonel, who, in the photograph, is a smudge of white moustache and spectacles, the entire earth a face looking upward for his inspection, the whole of Creation reduced to this missile: no sophistry in his body, whose one path is direct through the bones of the living. A year before this Brazilian trip, Nijinsky becomes a faun.

THE RIVER OF DOUBT

The photograph was taken by the President's son. Kermit, as a child, was sickly but had a flair for language and reading. As a freshman, he accompanied his father on a year-long expedition in Africa. For another expedition, to South America, he delayed his marriage. Like his father, he contracted malaria on the trip. But evidence suggests he downplayed his illness to save medicine for his father's use. There is a picture of Kermit in the Amazon with a beard and a hat, his eyes knowing and silent, but mainly silent. There is a picture too, from years earlier, of him holding his dog Jack, who looks at some force in the distance, as the ochre light of late afternoon cries on the scene. Although partridges steal one another's eggs, Leonardo Da Vinci, wrote, the young, when they have been hatched, always return to their true parents. When Kermit died in Alaska he never knew if he pleased his father.

ON THE HATRED OF V.S. NAIPAUL

Sunset and evening star, the portrait begins with unresolved
endings: the lash of empire, the contract of cane, begins with
forefathers and a father scribbling on water, begins with what
it means to sail beyond sunset: once across the Middle Passage,
once to England, once to the afterlife. What is the quiet limit
of the world? It is the idea of beginning again, beginning again
no matter what, closing doors, writing first sentences, opening
windows. Italian scientists have discovered that if you look
long enough into a mirror, strange faces will appear, multiple
deformations of one's own image: a parent with traits changed, an
unknown person, an old man, a child, a portrait of an ancestor, an
animal face – a cat, a pig, a lion, fantastical and monstrous beings.
But the portrait begins with you running through paragrass, away
from someone who touches you in secret and sets your world
alight. Once, I lived in a house where a child kept her favourite
book under a pillow, hoping to quench an ache with immaculate
prose. You could not live up to her. Yet, there is a cat in one of
your novels, in which the main character is named after stone, and
we know that behind your granite face, beneath the pentameter of
[and here is where I ask whether you deserve this poem; yet, what
is poetry if not a place to put doubt, the way Henry James put so
much uncertainty in *The Turn of the Screw*?] your iron-clad lines,
there is just rain and longing and a boy crying in the forest with
his sister, there is strength and weakness, joy and sorrow, love
and hate, poetry and sadism, the hope of early life, the cruelty of
old age, the perfected recto and verso of an imperfect self. What
does it mean to wound a world that wound you, a world which,
according to the Stoics, is what it is? And what is it this place in

which you now float like a bather in midsummer, Tobago, amid hot waves that dig out unseen trenches, and sometimes sand suspended in the backwash adds to the bar that forms the Nylon Pool and I imagine you not half-drowned, not wronged, not an agent provocateur but always treading salt water, resurfacing, sinking, sometimes aided by the tactile security of a parent's hand, sometimes thrillingly alone, in water that washes over your face, your eyes, so that the liquid becomes a lens and up there the clouds become JMW Turner's swirls. Sometimes, to stay alive in water you must fight your instinct, you must lean back, and gently extend your arms and legs, you must control your breathing and the denser the tears around you, the better your chances of transforming heavy burdens into a moving sleep. It is the fate of all writers to die, to be forgotten, to be reborn, to be held in the hands of others. Sleeping, I see you, dreaming your crossed positions, awaiting the embrace of water, awaiting another ending.

The Creature in the Flowers

Something or other lay in wait for him, amid the twists and the turns of the months and the years, like a crouching Beast in the Jungle. It signified little whether the crouching Beast were destined to slay him or to be slain. The definite point was the inevitable spring of the creature; and the definite lesson from that was that a man of feeling didn't cause himself to be accompanied by a lady on a tiger-hunt.

— Henry James, 'The Beast in the Jungle'

In 'The Beast in the Jungle', written at the threshold of the new century, the possibility of an embodied male-homosexual thematics has, I would like to argue, a precisely liminal presence...

— Eve Kosofsky Sedgwick, *Epistemology of the Closet*

CHAPTER I

What   startled him

                    was

his
            interest

                                in

                ecstasy

the dream of

the
                    great   poetry
                        that he needed
                                this impulse

                    a dog sniffing a

                            face

   affected him as the sequel of something of which he had lost the beginning. He knew it
as a continuation, but didn't know what it continued

                                                                        face to face
                  fumbling

          to   answer
                            to be
                                            satis-
fied

satisfied

                                  answer

                                      ghost

           he

                        penetrated   truth

                    red light, breaking at the close from under a low sombre sky, reached out in a long shaft and played over old wainscots, old tapestry, old gold, old colour.

                    the gap was filled up and the missing link
supplied
      He almost jumped at it

                  the

  flame

                      brilliant

                          They lingered together still

just waiting

                They looked at each other

Then they

were reduced for a few minutes more to wondering a little helplessly why their reunion had been so long averted. They didn't use that name for it, but their delay from minute to minute to join the others was a kind of confession that they didn't quite want it to be a failure.

He

He

He

They
They

He

touched him
he was

hot

He was ashamed
 he saw

 he

 he saw

 an ass
  just the sort of ass
 you have

 to know

 connect
 use

 eyes
 burnt

 a light broke

the blood slowly came to his face

                             he   came
                 he should

come

         he was lost in wonder and found himself

                 It took him but a moment, however, to feel it hadn't been, much as it had been a surprise

his secret had unaccountably faded from him

"So that I'm the only person who knows?"

"The only person in the world."

                 "I myself have never spoken. I've never, never repeated of you what you told me."

                     "And I never will."

"Please don't then. We're just right as it is."

"Oh I am," "if you are!" "Then you do still feel in the same way?"

He had thought of himself so long as abominably alone, and lo he wasn't alone a bit.

"What, exactly, was the account I gave—?"

"Of the way you did feel? Well, it was very simple. You said you had had from your earliest time, as the deepest thing within you, the sense of being kept for something rare and strange, possibly prodigious and terrible, that was sooner or later to happen to you, that you had in your bones the foreboding and the conviction of, and that would perhaps overwhelm you."

"Do you call that very simple?"

"It was perhaps because I seemed, as you spoke, to understand it."

"You do understand it?"

"You still have the belief?"

"Oh!" he exclaimed helplessly. There was too much to say.

"Whatever it's to be,"   "it hasn't yet come."

He shook his head in complete surrender now

"It's to be something you're merely to suffer?"

"Well, say to wait for—to have to meet, to face, to see suddenly break out in my life; possibly destroying all further consciousness, possibly annihilating me; possibly, on the other hand, only altering everything, striking at the root of all my world and leaving me to the consequences, however they shape themselves."

                        "Isn't what you describe perhaps but the expectation—or at any rate the sense of danger, familiar to so many people—of falling in love?"

"Of course," he said after a moment, "it strikes you

                                  love

        a cataclysm

                                  overwhelming

          love

                             God

a   coming violence

                      necessarily violent

                                    catastrophe

                                         gravity

          afraid

afraid

                              lunatic

                obsession

    afraid

CHAPTER II

The

    opportunities for meeting multiplied

in London

          They went together to the National Gallery and the South Kensington Museum, where, among vivid reminders, they talked of Italy at large—not now attempting to recover, as at first, the taste of their youth and their ignorance. That recovery, the first day had served its purpose well, had given them quite enough; so that they were no longer hovering about the head-waters of their stream, but had felt their boat pushed sharply off and down the current.

They were literally afloat together; for our gentleman this was marked He had with his own hands dug up this little hoard, brought to light—that is to within reach of the dim day constituted by their discretions and privacies—the object of value the hiding-place of which he had, after putting it into the ground himself, so strangely, so long forgotten. The rare luck of his having again just stumbled on the spot made him indifferent to any other question; he would doubtless have devoted more time to the odd accident of his lapse of memory if he hadn't been moved to devote so much to the sweetness, the comfort, as he felt, for the future, that this accident itself had helped to keep fresh. It had never entered into his plan that anyone should "know", and mainly for the reason that it wasn't in him to tell anyone. That would have been impossible, for nothing but the amusement of a cold world would have waited on it

                                    That the right person should know tempered the asperity of his secret

                                                               he was careful

                                      nobody knew

                        He hadn't disturbed people with the queerness   he had had moments of rather special temptation

                                                         they

would know

                              he promised himself to be much on
his guard. He was quite ready, none the less, to

                                    come into their
intercourse   he took
the intercourse itself for granted

                              a   Beast in
the Jungle. It signified little whether the   Beast were
destined to slay him or to be slain. The definite point was the in-
evitable spring of
      a man

                    on one's back

					face

												mind
			lap

								climax

		the consecration of the years

						the end of a period

		He
								against the rest of the world
													The rest
of the world of course thought him queer

took his gaiety from him—since it had to pass with them for gaiety—   took everything

                              never spoke of the
secret of his life except as "the real truth about you,"
                                                  the secret of

          him

his   happy perversion

               a   weight on his spirit
                           clever as he was, he fell short
              the secret of the difference

                         detachment

                 a long act of dissimulation. What it had come
to was that he wore a mask painted with the social simper, out
of the eye-holes of which there looked eyes of an expression not
in the least matching the other features. This the stupid world,
even after years, had never more than half discovered

                                                  straight

                    on a Sunday, at a season of thick fog and general
outward gloom   he   brought

                                                a small trinket
        it was

                                    for

                        me

            I

                              thought of

                                                        an
immense

                              Beast
            I was

                                                coming
                                                all the while

                                                                        year
after year, he brought
                                    intimate
                                                                things

                                                                        his
nervous moods
                    his whole middle life

            He

        touched

                        me   I was

                        free
                    afraid

                    I

                                        softly groaned, as with a gasp, half
spent, at the face

                                                        the
very eyes of the very Beast
                                    a sigh   rose from the
depths

    so full

                            in the dark

                                            I

       see I don't   I can't   I   know

                feel

                            everything

                                                 his

                            face
a confession

          some mystic line   secretly drawn
round
             himself

CHAPTER III

                                        I
came   again and again

                              always
awaited his pleasure

I never
        talked about

        my man

it was always as if

I   shouldn't

                                my

secret

I'm only, so far as people make out, ordinary

                                a

man like another   I am   not
compromised

                           enough

        grave pause, as if there might be a choice

It was into this going on as he was that they relapsed, and really for so long a time that the day inevitably came for a further sounding of their depths. These depths, constantly bridged over by a structure firm enough in spite of its lightness and of its occasional oscillation in the somewhat vertiginous air, invited on occasion, in the interest of their nerves, a dropping of the plummet and a measurement of the abyss. A difference had been made moreover, once for all, by the fact that

    within

        him

            circled   a distance that alternately
narrowed and widened

                                  a dread
of   some catastrophe—some catastrophe that yet
wouldn't at all be the catastrophe

        It was characteristic of the inner detachment he had hitherto so successfully cultivated and to which our whole account of him is a reference, it was characteristic that his complications, such as they were, had never yet seemed so as at this crisis to thicken about him, even to the point of making him ask himself if he were, by any chance, of a truth, within sight or sound, within touch or reach, within the immediate jurisdiction, of the thing that waited.

When the day came, as come it had to, that his friend confessed to him   a deep disorder in   blood, he felt somehow the shadow of a change and the chill of a shock. He immediately began to imagine mystical irresistible light

                                        a strange

                fire

a thick cluster

              a   long riddle

   a drop of   shadow

                  a

                                        long shadow

        Time
Time   fate

                                                        the
dark valley into which his path had taken

    He had   one desire

CHAPTER IV

Then

      the spring

                                              faded

                         nothing more to do

    There was something

              some-
thing

       everything

        sea-sand

       nothing

   couldn't

  a strange cold light

  of the season and the hour
 horrors

It deepened
                horrors

                                                          all
over

        frail and ancient
                              lost

                        smothered

                                                            surren-
    der

    no more light

  No no

forsaken

                            pain more   pleasure
cold charm

                         pity

                  light might   go out

                            suffer

      nothing

            something

    something

                Something

            nothing

a hole

                        door shut

                      door
shut   door open

   something

    once again, always
      too late   diminished
  distance

                unspoken

                    He had
        fireless

  something

                without consequence

                                            failed
       Something
                  closing

                                        turned off and

sunk back

                die without   light

                        as if some difference had been
made
                               nothing

happened

CHAPTER V

He

                              He
he   him   his
                                              he
              he   he
          him
him   him   him   he
   him
              his   he
              He   he

                                      his
                                   he
              He
He
         he
                                          he
                       his
                                            him
              He

     he

              he
                          him

·　　　　　him

　　　　　　　　　　　　　　　　　　　　his
　　　　his

　　　　　　He
　　　　he

　　　　him

　　　he

Face to face　　　　　　　he
　　　he

He　　　himself

　　　　　　　　　　　　　　　　　him

    him

                        His

  he

He   his
            him   he
                  he
                            him
              he
   his

He

              him   dream
  dreams

He
  dreams

                        him

me

He   his
                    him   his
        he   he

                                He

                            he   he

    him

                he

him him

him

I

I

I

he

he
I I

                        I
                him

    he

                him he

                                he

                him

                                his

                        him   his
        he
                            him
him

            his
            he

                                    He
                                    he

        him He   he
he
                        him   he
                        he

                                he

                his

                he
            his   his
                    his
his

he   he

He

he
                    He

   Beast   his
                                        Beast

                              his
                              him   He

           he
      his

                              himself
      his

                        Beast
                  He
                                 him   himself

               his
   him   his

         he   his
         He
   his   his   his

                                    his   he

                        him his
          him   he
                        him
                        him   he
he
              he

                                    He
              he
                    he   his
              his
                          him
                      him
                  he
he
                          he   he
                                  he
him
              him
              he   he
                                his

                                he
                          himself   he
                                He

                              his
              his
          his   he
      him   He

                              him
                                        him   He
                          light

CHAPTER VI

He   visited

      a man who had known what

                                       he had lived

for so many years

                The   truth was

                                                he

was

the

creature

                          in

                the   flowers

      It   grew

    this garden
                             It was

                an open page

                          in which he

could lose himself
                                                                his
hand
                    his younger self

his

                    hair

                                        his ache

                                                        the
leaves

                        bowed back   clustered

                        near   the face

              at the other   himself

              the path
                    his

                                                  men

                                                  his

                              sorrow

                                                            his

                                                          pas-
sion

                      extraordinary

                                wonder
wound it   healed

                        passion
            passion

            flame
                                    train   fire

torch

 illumination
blazed

 the open page   his story

 the Beast

the   Beast

ACKNOWLEDGEMENTS

'Bestiary in Which I Have Nothing Left Anymore' contains two lines that riff off Burna Boy's 'Alone'.

'Bestiary Set in the Port of Spain General Hospital' contains a phrase borrowed from Denise Levertov.

'Prospect Cottage, 2022' is inspired by Wallace Stevens.

'The Jaguar' and 'The River of Doubt' refer to the infamous photograph of Theodore Roosevelt Jr and a jaguar killed on a hunting expedition to Brazil between 1913 and 1914, taken by his son, Kermit.

'The Creature in the Flowers' is an erasure of Henry James' novella 'The Beast in the Jungle', first published in *The Better Sort* (London: Methuen, 1903). Visual elements by the author.

Poems previously appeared in *The Lincoln Review*, the *Gingo Ecopoetry Anthology 2022* (contest judges Linda Gregerson, Sean Hewitt, and Karen McCarthy Woolf, Poetry School, 2023), *Masculinity: an anthology of modern voices* (edited by Rick Dove, Aaron Kent, and Stuart McPherson, Broken Sleep Books, 2024), and *Dream Latin: Writing the Subconscious* (edited by Aaron Kent and Jacqueline Yallop, Broken Sleep, 2024). Special thanks to Aaron Kent, Charlie Baylis, Andil Gosine, Simon Savidge, Ronald Spooner, Stuart McPherson, Daniele Pantano, Kenneth Ramchand and Lisa Allen-Agostini.

LAY OUT YOUR UNREST